Our Sun

William B. Rice

Consultants

Sally Creel, Ed.D.
Curriculum Consultant

Leann Iacuone, M.A.T., NBCT, ATC
Riverside Unified School District

Jill Tobin
California Teacher of the Year
Semi-Finalist
Burbank Unified School District

Image Credits: pp.16–17 Emmanuel LATTES/Alamy;
pp.12–13 Sjoerd van der Wal/Getty Images; pp.20–21
(illustrations) Chris Sabatino; all other images
from Shutterstock.

Library of Congress Cataloging-in-Publication Data

Rice, William B. (William Benjamin), 1961- author.
  Our sun / William B. Rice; consultants, Sally Creel, Ed.D.,
curriculum consultant, Leann Iacuone, M.A.T., NBCT, ATC,
Riverside Unified School District, Jill Tobin, California
Teacher of the Year semi-finalist, Burbank Unified
School District.
       pages cm
     Summary: "The sun gives us warmth. The sun gives
us light. It makes the seasons change. Our sun is very
important!"— Provided by publisher.
     Audience: K to grade 3.
     Includes index.
     ISBN 978-1-4807-4570-4 (pbk.)
     ISBN 978-1-4807-5060-9 (ebook)
  1. Sun—Juvenile literature. I. Title.
     QB521.5.R534 2015
     523.7—dc23
                                        2014013158

Teacher Created Materials
5301 Oceanus Drive
Huntington Beach, CA 92649-1030
http://www.tcmpub.com
ISBN 978-1-4807-4570-4

Table of Contents

3

Day and Night

In the morning, the bright **sun** wakes us.

This is daytime.

Dawn

Dawn is the morning, just before we see the sun.

Through the day, the sun looks higher in the sky.

We feel its **warmth** and see its light.

In the evening, the sun seems to sink in the sky.

Darkness comes and nighttime begins.

Dusk

Dusk is the evening, just after the sun goes down.

The night is not warm like the day.

Hello, Moon

Sometimes, we see the **moon** at night.

This girl wears a coat at night to keep warm.

The sun makes the warmth.

She does not need a coat on a hot day. The sun keeps her warm.

Seasons and Weather

Through the year, the **length** of the day changes.

The **weather** changes, too.

Dark clouds may mean that cooler weather is coming.

In summer, days are longer.

7 PM in the summer

In winter, days are shorter.

7 PM in the winter

Summer is mainly warm.

summer

Winter is mainly cold.

winter

Seasons Change

The **seasons** change as parts of Earth get more sun than others.

Our Important Sun

The sun warms and lights Earth.
It helps make the seasons.

It is important for life on Earth!

Let's Do Science!

How does the sun affect objects?
Try this and see!

What to Get

- ○ black rock

- ○ ice cube

- ○ newspaper

- ○ paper and pencil

- ○ timer

- ○ unwrapped chocolate bar

What to Do

1 Lay the newspaper on the ground on a hot day.

2 Place each object on the newspaper.

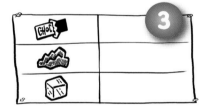

3 Draw a picture of each object in a chart.

4 Watch the objects for about 30 minutes. Then, write what happened to the object. Touch each item and describe how it feels, too. (Be careful of the hot rock!)

Glossary

length—the distance from one end to the other

moon—the biggest bright object we see in the sky at night

seasons—the four different times of year marked by changing weather and length of day

sun—the star that gives us light and heat

warmth—the feeling of heat

weather—the way the air, the clouds, and the sky look and feel

Index

Your Turn!

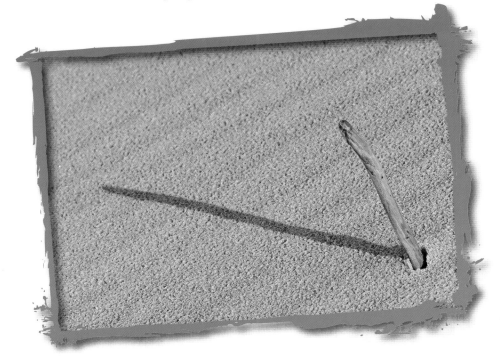

Sun Shadow

Get a long stick and place it in the ground. Throughout the day, mark the end of the stick's shadow. At the end of the day, what do you notice about the marks?